W9-ATZ-253

Pebble Plus

FAVORITE DESIGNER DOGS

You'll Love Labradoodles

by Erin Edison

Gail Saunders-Smith PhD,
Consulting Editor

CAPSTONE PRESS
a capstone imprint

Pebble Plus is published by Capstone Press,
1710 Roe Crest Drive, North Mankato, Minnesota 56003
www.capstonepub.com

Library of Congress Cataloging-in-Publication Data
Edison, Erin.
  You'll love Labradoodles / Erin Edison.
    pages cm—(Favorite designer dogs)
  Includes bibliographical references and index.
  ISBN 978-1-4914-0570-3 (hb)—ISBN 978-1-4914-0604-5 (eb)—ISBN 978-1-4914-0638-0 (pb)
  1. Labradoodle—Juvenile literature. I. Title.
  SF429.L29E35 2015
  636.72'8—dc23

2014001832

Editorial Credits
Erika L. Shores, editor; Kyle Grenz, designer; Katy LaVigne, production specialist

Photo Credits
Capstone Studio: Karon Dubke, 9, 17, 21; Dreamstime: Erik Lam, 5, Judith Dzierzawa, 5; Shutterstock: Claudia Naerdemann, 19, Gordo25, 15, Steven Belanger, 13, Ysbrand Cosijn, cover, 7, zstock, 1; SuperStock/Juniors, 11

Design Elements
Shutterstock: Julynx

Note to Parents and Teachers

The Favorite Designer Dogs series supports national science standards related to life science. This book describes and illustrates Labradoodles, a cross between a Labrador retriever and a poodle. The images support early readers in understanding the text. The repetition of words and phrases helps early readers learn new words. This book also introduces early readers to subject-specific vocabulary words, which are defined in the Glossary section. Early readers may need assistance to read some words and to use the Table of Contents, Glossary, Read More, Internet Sites, and Index sections of the book.

Printed in the United States of America in North Mankato, Minnesota.
042014   008087CGF14

Table of Contents

What Is a Labradoodle?

Labradoodles are designer dogs. Designer dogs are made up of two breeds. Also called doodles, these dogs blend a Labrador retriever and a poodle.

poodle

Labrador retriever

The Labradoodle Look

Labradoodles look friendly and sweet. Their ears lie flat on their heads. Their eyes are shaped like almonds.

Like poodles, doodles can be standard, medium, or miniature in size. A doodle stands between 14 and 24 inches (36 and 61 centimeters) tall.

Doodles can have one of three coat types. Fleece coats are silky soft. Wool coats are thick and curly. Hair coats are straighter than the others.

hair coat

Labradoodles can be many colors. Most doodles are black or a golden tan. Doodles can also be red or brown.

Puppy Time

Doodle puppies take one
to two years to reach full size.
Doodles live 12 to 14 years.

Caring for Labradoodles

Brushing a doodle weekly
is important. Doodles with
hair coats need more brushing
because they shed more.

Doodles are full of energy.
They need walks every day.
Doodles also like to play.
Playing fetch is a fun way
to exercise a doodle.

Darling Doodles

Sweet, smart Labradoodles like
being with people and other dogs.
Doodles are happy members
of many families.

Glossary

coat—an animal's hair or fur

breed—a certain kind of animal within an animal group

energy—the strength to do active things without getting tired

fleece—soft, fluffy hair like that of a sheep

miniature—smaller than the usual size

shed—to drop or fall off

Read More

Bozzo, Linda. *I Like Labrador Retrievers!* Discover Dogs with the American Canine Association. Berkeley Heights, N.J.: Enslow Publishers, 2012.

Owen, Ruth. *Labradoodles.* Designer Dogs. New York: PowerKids Press, 2013.

Shores, Erika L. *All About Poodles.* Dogs, Dogs, Dogs. North Mankato, Minn.: Capstone Press, 2013.

Internet Sites

FactHound offers a safe, fun way to find Internet sites related to this book. All of the sites on FactHound have been researched by our staff.

Here's all you do:

Visit *www.facthound.com*

Type in this code: 9781491405703

Super-cool stuff! Check out projects, games and lots more at
www.capstonekids.com

Index

Word Count: 188
Grade: 1
Early-Intervention Level: 14

24